ISBN 9781791796266

Independently published
Layout & Cover Designed by: Bilal Rasheed

CONTENTS

Foreword

Over the last few years, I have met hundreds of graduates from different programs, all of whom have a sincere desire to work well, find a role that they love, and earn a good salary. Some find their feet from day one, some take 6-12 months, but many find themselves at the end of the program still unsure of what to do and wondering if they are making a mistake choosing a particular path. I certainly felt this myself and struggled to apply the advice given to me, which seemed to conflict with other people's advice. It was confusing and frustrating, and I felt like the majority of my success depended on my boss and how he rated my performance. Coming directly out of a degree, which had each semester pre-planned, into an environment where everything was open and left up to me to decide was unnerving. Many of the books I read or talks I heard throughout my time as a graduate were by people who were years ahead of me and had found their purpose at work. It wasn't what I needed at the time; rather, I was desperate to hear from other successful graduates who had found their paths as they were in the thick of it. Those feelings gave rise to the thoughts that brought me to write this book, dealing with each of the areas that are key to being successful both in the workplace and your life, from someone who has very recently been there themselves.

I have not met my career goals and am still at the earliest stage of my working life. However, I define success as coming off the graduate program having learned as much as I could, getting involved in my work, creating lasting and true relationships, putting my name out there and being known for something.

I do not define it as what my title is, nor salary. On this basis, I am truly successful and want to share the strategies I have learnt and used along the way. I do not pretend to know more than the next person, but I have a love for observing people, reading books from the masters, and finding ways to use these qualities in my daily work life to maximize my influence at an infant stage of my career. There will always be people smarter, more efficient and strategic than me, but isn't that what it's all about anyway? Without people like that, why bother taking the time to work on yourself to become a better performer and colleague?

This book is your handbook to the success I've defined above, and I encourage you to use it as a continual companion. When you feel like the work you are doing is not meaningful or taking you anywhere, pick up the "Serve" chapter and remember that it is very rarely about what you do but how you do it. Leaders arise from these situations when they can turn the mundane into shortcuts to success.

When you feel like you may crumble under the anxiety of an interview for the role of your dreams, re-read the "Interview Guide" and redirect the focus away from yourself so that you can think clearly and be present.

Ultimately, take ownership of the work. Feel frustrated when things don't work out for everyone, feel excited when there is a win. This does not mean take on all the stress and stay up all night worrying. It means let yourself be connected to the larger goals of the business or team, and understand the part you have to play in it. When you do, you will be well on the path to standing out, known for your work ethic and authenticity.

The first three chapters will deal with topics that you have heard many times over. However, they do not contain conventional wisdom and will hopefully encourage you to find out more about any of the new mindsets you come across. There is so much that can be written on leadership, interview tactics, and networking; however, putting that all on paper was not my intention. I want to outline key principles that you can take and make your own, just as I have on my own journey. Mindsets have become more important to me than having a perfect strategy, as they underpin the way you look at everything that happens to you. With the correct mindset, you can turn almost any setback into an opportunity to evolve.

If a topic piques your interest, flip to the back of the book and note the resources associated with it. Go deep, read, learn and I promise you, results will follow.

SERVING DOESN'T MAKE YOU A SERVANT, IT MAKES YOU A LEADER

01

Serve

Not a word that is used a lot when starting out your career. I generally heard things like *networking, prioritize, under promise & over deliver, future leader, mentor,* and *diversify.* Society tends to see the word *"serve"* as a disempowered state, something that the lowest in the hierarchy do for those higher up in the food chain. Allow me to challenge that and show you that this is one of the most powerful weapons you possess as a graduate.

When I was studying, like many other students, I had a part-time job in a tea retailer in the outer suburbs of Melbourne. The company prided itself on customer service and we were told clearly that no matter how wrong they were, the customer was always right. For the five years I was there, this included providing discounts on items that never existed, giving more than the three maximum samples, returns on non-returnable items, and much more. I would be lying if I told you that I understood this concept. The customers were clearly misunderstanding the signs and were too lazy to take note of prices. Why was this our problem?

A few years into the job, it was quiet and I was alone one Monday morning after opening up the shop. A lady came in who didn't look like she was in a hurry and was happily browsing. I was in a great mood, so I offered her some freshly brewed tea that I had made for myself that morning. With a surprised and excited look, she accepted. I gave it to her in a beautiful ceramic tumbler, which she instantly cupped in her hands and continued to walk around the store.

Shortly after, she returned to the counter and bought the largest size of the tea I had offered her. We spoke more about it as we drank it together, about the floral notes, the lightness, and of course, the most important one, with or without milk? I threw in three more samples of teas I thought she would like.

A week later, she came back for the three I'd given her, plus any others I recommended. Over the following years, she became my customer, someone who valued my opinion and trusted that I had her interest at heart. This happened many times during my time there, which led me to notice the following:

1. When I served her, I enjoyed it, which attracted more customers
2. I received loyalty as a result of my service
3. The company received revenue as a result of her loyalty

Serve someone by solving their problem and you will create value. Create value and you will create profit. Service is a crucial part of the success of both you and your company.

When I left retail and entered the graduate program, I took for granted how much I learnt being on the sales floor for five years. Having worked out how to create consistent sales and a solid customer base, I disregarded these skills in the corporate workplace. After all, who cares about retail experience? It wasn't part of my "career" but was just a way to make enough cash to send me to Europe once a semester. The truth was, these skills translated beautifully into my job and enabled me to be successful with both people and my work. Let's break it down further.

During my time as a graduate, I noticed many conversations during the Friday afternoon beer o'clock that revolved around "I don't know why I'm the one who has to sit on Excel all day", "I should have been in that meeting", "my team is useless", "I haven't had a 1:1 with my manager in weeks", and on and on and on. After all, aren't we the top 1% of the 1% in the country and the future leaders of this company? How could I be spending the last four months taking minutes or documenting processes? Don't they know how much more I can give?

In my admittedly short career, I have seen cohorts of graduates come through with similar outlooks on their rotations. Whether this stems from unrealistic expectations that make us frustrated with the work, I don't know. What I do know is that many waste opportunities that they may never see again as their heads are down in the weeds of "boring work". We have come into programs all over the world by being the best, only to find a less fulfilling environment than we had hoped for. By the way, this is not the case with everyone all the time. If you haven't felt this yet, keep these principles in your pocket for when that day arrives.

I do believe there is a solution which can be found in this concept. *Anteambulo: the one who clears the path.* Originating in Roman culture, this role belonged to the person who would go before their patron (swap out for boss or client)and do whatever was necessary to ensure that they had a smooth journey.

If you can master this concept, the world will become your oyster, full of opportunities to learn skills and figure out your leadership style. The strategy boils down to this: *find and make canvases for others to paint on.* This is not simply making others look good but taking on the grunt work they would normally do so that they can focus on their strengths and shine. By doing so, you can achieve a couple of things.

First, if you have a god-complex, this will teach you that you are not above any work or anyone. The sooner this is learnt, the sooner you can graduate from this phase and become a leader that inspires and extracts the best out of everyone around you.

To illustrate this, I only need to take you back a couple of months. There was an event that I was asked to moderate that had senior executives from various companies on the panel. As I walked in, I noticed they were all just sitting by themselves, far apart and on their phones. It was an awkward environment.

One of the panelists got up and walked over to the event coordinator, asking where the chairs were, and joked that they were going to have to stand up all night. Overhearing this, I jumped up to find five chairs and brought them in one by one, as they were quite heavy. The coordinator followed suit and helped me, but not one of the panelists asked nor attempted to help, even as they saw us doing multiple trips. They must have assumed I was part of the event set-up team and figured this was my mistake in the first place.

When the room filled up and the night kicked off, each panelist was introduced to the audience. Finally, my name was called, along with a very flattering introduction as moderator. When I sat down in one of the chairs I had brought in myself, some of the panel members looked at me with disbelief. The assumption that I must just be a helper because I had done the "grunt" work (literally—I had been grunting, they were so heavy) was blown out of the water as they realized that I was actually hosting the event. Their reaction taught me something important: Behaving like you are above something because you are overqualified or you think there is someone else whose job it is to do it is not the sign of a leader. I felt a great amount of ownership that night, and satisfaction knowing that I had shown people what it means to serve. This is such a small example and by no means is it me trying to imply all executives are like this, because they're not. I wanted to add this story here to show you that you can quickly develop a reputation of leadership by turning the "norm" on its head. It is so easy to shine in a world where people wait for someone else to take action or believe it's not their job to do something. With just a few acts of initiative that serve, you can inspire people at every level by demonstrating true leadership.

Second, you don't know what you don't know, so don't assume you know. By allowing those around you to shine, you can watch and learn how they operate without making the mistakes yourself. This could be one of the greatest shortcuts to success in this book.

We all know that the more information you can gather around something, the better you will understand it, and therefore the better decisions you will make around it. I don't see leadership as being any different. Aside from throwing yourself into books and articles on how to be a great leader, watching people go about it daily was what actually encouraged me to write this book. I had observed many styles of leadership and decision making by offering myself up to do the grunt work they didn't want to do. Napoleon Hill put it perfectly: *"Most great leaders begin in the capacity of followers."* This means that there is a way to follow *intelligently,* and in fact, the ones that do find themselves in positions of leadership rapidly through observation of those around them.

I believe people are inherently good, but in a culture where he who is on stage or presenting is the one who gets all the credit, it's easy to fall into the same patterns and fight for the recognition. If you master this strategy and continuously ask yourself, "What can I do for this person to make their life easier?" you will fast-track your learning curve and set yourself up for success by playing the long game.

If you will allow me, I would like to take this one step further. Dr. John Demartini is a world-renowned expert in human behavior, and has spent decades observing and writing about how we can achieve success and fulfill our purpose on earth. He writes about two parts of our brain: the executive mind and the animalistic mind. While the animalistic mind is concerned with survival and short-term outcomes, the executive mind has far-sighted vision and well-defined strategies to execute that vision. If you take a moment to think about the people in your team or management chain, I'm sure you can see both of these qualities playing out in different ways, as well as within yourself.

The greatest leaders on earth have harnessed their "executive mind" and made decisions that transcend the here and now. That is why someone like Warren Buffet can watch multiple stock market crashes yet be confident in his investments over the long term and continue to make profit regardless of the economic climate.

Doing the grunt work and taking on extra things that clear the way for your boss or team is harnessing your executive mind. You have the capacity to do this, unlike many other people, because you know that this is an investment towards your future. You are happy to go beyond your "job description" because you see that you are increasing your skill set and observing how those around you operate. You take note of what you see working and what you see not working. You listen to how people react to rude emails and you note that you will never write an email in that tone when you lead a team.

Another way to fast-track your learning is to take responsibility for *everything*. Earlier in this chapter, I spoke of how I used to hear graduates complaining about the lack of work or not having enough face time with their manager. Some saw their development going only as far as their manager would be inclined to. For example, if they had a nurturing one who took them under their wing and brought them along to everything, only then could they develop and learn. What this tells me is that they (and myself, at the time) didn't take responsibility for things being the way they are. I'm not saying that everything that you are unhappy with is your fault, but by becoming a victim, you give that power over to someone else. The minute you take responsibility for your part to play in everything by *default,* you immediately give yourself the power to change it.

Every 6-12 months, we interview graduates to come into our team as their first role coming off the program. There have been times where we've had more than 10 and of course had to let most of them know that they were not successful. Many times, when this happened, I was approached for a follow-up chat about what they could have done better and any advice for the future. I thought this was a fantastic initiative, and I was looking forward to helping them in anyway possible. There were two types in this scenario: the first would begin to listen to my feedback but then would get defensive and explain why they failed. Perhaps it was that they did not really want the role, or that they felt the questions were too hard. The second whipped out their notebooks and wrote down everything I said, nodded and asked me to explain further. Their ability to receive feedback well and take responsibility of the outcome, I believe, is what will make this group become leaders much quicker than the first. Taking ownership over career outcomes and making the most of every opportunity to learn, grow, and fine-tune your strategy is the key to success. I see so many graduates, past and present, go in circles making the same mistakes and getting the same outcomes because they never took the time to evaluate where they went wrong or sought out someone to guide them.

Tim Ferriss has an incredible interview with Jocko Willink, a Special Forces operative who led the most decorated SEAL unit from the Iraq war. His bestseller can be found in the booklist at the back of this book. Something he said stood out to me and changed how I looked at my current state at work:

You can't blame your boss for not giving you the support you need. Plenty of people will say, 'It's my boss's fault.' No, it's actually your fault because you haven't educated him, you haven't influenced him, you haven't explained to him in a manner he understands why you need this support that you need. That's extreme ownership. Own it all.

So how does this relate back to us? If your goal is to become a leader, creating positive outcomes for your company and enabling those around you to work at their full potential, it starts now. It starts by you embracing the canvas strategy and doing the grunt work to prop up those around you and clear the way for them. Once you recognize the power of doing the things no one wants to do, you become grateful for it, and that is when it will stop becoming grunt work and instead become a clear pathway to success. Because, ultimately, the one who clears the way controls the direction.

Going back to my personal story at the beginning of this chapter, with the canvas strategy in mind, can you see how powerful putting people first can be?

Serving is a weapon, not an act of low self-worth.

Learn the above principles, read about those who mastered it and those who wrote about it, apply it in your day to day, and see how your results become transformed.

The quality of your life is determined by the quality of the questions you ask yourself

⌐ What gaps or inefficiencies are present within my team that I can recommend or build fixes for?

⌐ Do I understand the broader strategy and my role within it?

⌐ Does my ego get in the way of contributing to the vision of my team?

⌐ What are the pain points of my manager and how can I ease them?

⌐ What skills or techniques am I observing from people that I can apply later on? Are they effective or not?

⌐ Have I blamed someone or something for my dissatisfaction or rejection? What was my role in it and how can I make sure I learn from it?

NETWORKING

THE KEY TO NETWORKING IS GO NARROW, GO DEEP

02

Advanced Networking

The one area where "go big or go home" doesn't work. In fact, if you go big, you *will* go home...without contacts.

This chapter is also served with a side of "infatuations and resentments" that will help you create a balanced view of your goals and re-define your definition of success.

Networking was the single most mentioned word I can remember for my first two years of my career. For something that is talked about so much, I cannot believe how little is said on how to actually make it work for you. In some interpretations of networking I've seen, that person was better off not starting a conversation at all.

The first thing I want to say is that this has nothing to do with being an introvert or extrovert. Just because someone else is more natural at or comfortable with striking up a conversation with a stranger, be it a manager or peer, that does not make them a better networker than you. What does matter is your ability to create an authentic and lasting relationship that serves both of you.

Let's start with a typical example of how a you may have tackled your first month of work. With your head full of the importance of networks and contacts, you go into every conversation ticking off things in your head like "what area are they working in", "who do they report to", "do I want to work in this area", "does their job sound interesting". By doing this, you restrict your interest in the person to revolving only around their job, hoping that down the line, you can rely on them to open a door for you. This is a temporary and shallow style of networking and will not serve you when that person moves to a different company or role.

The key to networking is go narrow, go deep.

When we all began looking for roles during our rotations, everyone went about this differently, with some loading up their diaries with work coffees with various managers or ex-grads. Some put all their eggs into one basket and did everything they could to make sure the role they were currently rotating in was what they could stay in. The first group tends to experience what I call "1:1 fatigue", getting confused with all the opinions and suggestions and feeling paralyzed with indecision for where they should go next. I experienced this at its worst when I was looking for a permanent role. My mistake was asking several competing teams their advice, which left me with disappointing reviews of the teams I wanted to work with and feeling frustrated and hopeless that I would ever be happy in a role. I forgot that when you go broad, you carry a greater risk of conflicting advice given by people who themselves may not be happy in their role and are projecting that onto you. I began to *prioritize the advice of those who had the results I wanted.*

Going narrow means being picky with the people you allow to speak into your situation, choosing only those that you consider successful and have the career or traits you aspire to. They are usually the ones that are transparent with the good and the bad, and encourage you to have realistic expectations. They will also be the ones that you don't only need today but see value in for the next few stages of your career, and even when you move on from the company to the next thing. So, if your diary is full of 1:1's and you have a list of people that you go back to for advice every step of the way, get critical on them and narrow it down to a handful that you value above the rest. Once you have the list, work at it, water it, and grow it. Go deep. This is where you move beyond "work" and get to know them as human beings with personal goals and interests.

I know so many grads who spend their working hours getting 1:1 fatigue, but then their Friday nights or lunch times are spent around other graduates. I am the first to say this is not a bad thing, as some of my closest friends who came to my wedding are from the program. I believe it is important to be respected and liked amongst your graduate peers, as you will all eventually move onto other industries or companies where your network could multiply quicker than ever. However, I recognized that right now, this was not the type of networking I needed. I didn't have a view of what I wanted to become or what it would take to become a leader, so I had to seek out people that had achieved what I wanted and work to build a lasting relationship with them.

Networking isn't just about growing your contacts or people you can reach out to when you need advice or opportunities, but it gives you the chance to peek into the lives of people that you wouldn't normally have access to, allowing you to get valuable insights that can have a massive impact on your decision making. I cannot emphasize this enough, and I hope this story inspires you to go out and cultivate relationships with people that you want to become, so that you can be efficient with your emotions and define your version of success early on.

There was a leader within my area of the business whom I immediately found myself in awe of for his ability to connect with people and put them at ease whilst leading a highly technical and complex business. So many on that level tend to make you feel awkward around them, as your lives have very little in common, with different challenges, different goals, and different peers.

Whenever I was around him, he leveled the playing field and was comfortable talking about things that most graduates are not privy to. Very quickly, he began to inspire me, and I couldn't wait to help his vision come to life. In my short time in corporate life, I saw that there are not many leaders who are this transparent and highly intelligent, which is probably why he made such a big impact on me.

One afternoon, we were out for team drinks, and as conversations started breaking off around the table, we began to have one of our own. I've always been curious about business leadership and what challenges you face once your role makes you the face of an entire business. Fortunately, he was the type to enjoy this too, so we talked about his relationship with his peers and his manager, and to the rest of the company. Through conversations like these, I was able to build a good relationship between us, where I was always keen to understand what being in his position was like, and allowed him to share his learning's with someone he wouldn't normally interact with in his day to day. He freely spoke to me about his challenges and frustrations, allowing me to see another side to our business, where one has to fight for their team and resources at a level where everyone is competing for the same.

These conversations are the best way to destroy any infatuations you may have about leadership roles. The quickest way for you to become disheartened with a company or role is through infatuations that get challenged, which then turn into resentment. I've seen so many people who have joined a company based on infatuations and ideals of what working there will be like, ignoring any signs that say the opposite. I've definitely been there when it comes to people I've dated (love is oh so blind) and have not had an open mind to facts that may be contrary to my beliefs.

When infatuation turns into resentment, the mind gets closed off to any positives that contradict this new belief. This can translate as someone quitting unexpectedly due to some seemingly small incident or breaking up with someone over a small argument. Neither is true, which makes this way of living very emotionally exhausting and could lead to burnouts, anxiety, or missed opportunities.

Talking to people in the role that you want and asking them the right questions is a great shortcut to finding out if it is actually what you want. Ask them what their biggest challenges are, who or what blocks them from doing their job, or what having their peers is like. Find out all the negatives to balance out your infatuations, so that your internal pendulum becomes balanced and at rest. The times that I've done this, I've experienced a huge amount of gratitude for my current position and freedom, as well as having a realistic view of the goals that I want to achieve. You save untold amounts of emotional energy by avoiding getting angry over organizational changes, managers moving on, or your role changing, and instead, you can think clearly and objectively about what is right for you.

From this, my definition of success changed dramatically. Before understanding the personal and professional toil a role like his could bring, I wanted to be him. I defined success as working myself into that role before I turned 40, and inspiring others to work alongside me to bring my own vision to life. It was only through my relationship with him that I saved myself years of frustration working towards a role that I did not have a balanced perception of.

I hope that this is something that you will work to do for yourself, as the last thing I would want is for you to base your working life around a goal that you have not looked at from all angles. You can start this process by reading the biographies of people who have succeeded in business and/or leadership, make notes of the aspects of their lives that you consider negative, and re-assess whether or not you would still accept this in light of what you now know. By the way, this exercise is applicable in all areas of life, including relationships, health, and wealth. When you begin to neutralize your infatuations in these areas and have a balanced view on all your goals, you will experience such a high level of certainty within yourself and will therefore seize opportunities that will get you where you want to go.

Before we move on, I want to introduce you to the concept of networking via osmosis, a way to develop your "secret sauce". So far, we've discussed the importance of having a narrow but solid list of people that you have cultivated strong relationships with. This is imperative for your overall career development and high-level networking, but there is also another kind that has more to do with your daily working routine and plays significantly into your personal branding, a topic we will deal with later on. When you begin to apply the principles in "Serve"and start to volunteer totake on more of the work that nobody wants to do, pretty quickly, people will take notice.

For example, when I was in one of my rotations, there was new software to store internal documents, and no one had taken the time to understand it. It was horribly laid out, ugly, and full of clunky data and illogical functions. For almost three months, I was taking online courses to work out how to make the best use of this system and migrating documents over to it, painfully and manually. Safe to say, I felt low, bored, and irrelevant.

I started to catch myself wondering why I had bothered with a degree that took up so much of my life, just to sit here and be someone else's slave. Looking back, it wasn't actually that bad, but those emotions were real in that moment.

It wasn't too long after that that I had people being referred to me from other teams who couldn't figure out how to use the system either. I would help them and then get many more requests after that person recommended me to their colleagues. Now, I've seen this play out where someone becomes known as a spreadsheet monkey and is asked to continue doing the same thing because they are too good at it. That is not what I want for you. I want you to realize that when you commit to doing your best in the small and insignificant things, people take notice and you will be known as a dependable and consistent performer. Remember the concept of osmosis in high school, where a substance will tend to diffuse through a permeable membrane in order to balance itself? Visualize this process when you think about how your day-to-day work can play out and expand your network dramatically. There have been countless times where my manager has not been able to make something happen, but through my vast knowledge of people all over the business, I knew who to contact to get it done. This is so critical in bringing value to your team, and creating value is the most sought after commodity in business.

The quality of your life is determined by the quality of the questions you ask yourself

⌐ Who is on my list of go-to people when I need advice or support at work?

⌐ Do they have the results that I want?

⌐ Who are the 3 or 5 people that are in the role that I want in the next 5-10 years?

⌐ How can I develop a relationship with these people?

⌐ Have I been objective in both the positives and negatives of my goals?

⌐ What connections have I made outside my team through my daily work? [make a list of these people and their teams and use it as your secret sauce to get things done]

MAKE
YOURSELF
MEMORABLE
CREATE
DEMAND

03

Interview Guide

I spent weeks trying to find a better title, to no avail. Pop this one into Google and you'll have no shortage of advice, dos and don'ts, corporate images of people looking like they would rather glue their eyes shut than be there...super inspirational.

So much has been said on this topic that I believe it has made something that should be natural and simple into something extremely complex, nerve racking, and dreaded. Let me save you time and summarize everything you'll find on the internet:

1. Be on time & plan your journey
2. Dress appropriately
3. Research the company (financials, strategy, performance, etc.)
4. Prepare stories to answer the questions with
5. Know your strengths and weaknesses
6. Prepare answers to the most-asked behavioral and situational questions
7. Have good posture
8. Be attentive
9. Look interested
10. ...I can't do this anymore, let's move on

At this point in your career, you would have already been through one (at least) of these and have come across this advice already. And, assuming you now find yourself in a graduate program, you must have done some or all of these things! What I want to do is help you stand head and shoulders above your peers and help you to create demand for yourself. It is fundamental that you find ways to make this work for you, so that you have *choice* after the program, or at any stage of your career, which is key to finding the right role.

Growing up with parents who were incredible public speakers, some of their techniques became second nature to me. I credit this a lot with my success in interviews, about 17 to date. The key is that I naturally tend towards building authentic relationships with people as fast as possible, and the interview room is no exception.

Let's look at the physiology of someone heading into a job interview. You are standing outside the room waiting, you arrived ahead of schedule (thanks to the #1 rule), and now find yourself going over random details in your head and possibly scouting out other applicants around you. You sit there stewing in the nervous tension that has built up inside of you all day, compounded if your slot is late afternoon! Your interviewer comes out and calls your name, looks at you and asks you to follow them. You're forcing a smile and trying to be friendly, maybe asking awkward questions like "you must have had a busy day", or "wow, you must be back to back". You sit down across from your interviewers and either sit there in silence while they organize themselves or continue asking awkward, unnatural questions.

Now I'm not saying any of this is bad; in fact, it's impressive that you even tried to make conversation! Many people I've interviewed or observed haven't even done that. However, this book isn't for the basics. It is designed to make you *memorable* so when someone asks your interviewer how the day went, they respond with, "Great! I already have someone in mind."

The key to a great interview is to not treat it like an interview but a genuine conversation between two people to find out if your talents, skills, and personality are compatible with their needs. The more authentic, engaging, and passionate you come across, the higher your success rate will be. Remember that the person sitting opposite you is not a robot. In fact, they can be just as nervous as you are! They are human and are *wanting* to hire someone, or else they wouldn't be in the room with you. Of course, this needs to be altered for highly technical interviews where your skills—i.e. coding, design, and specialized knowledge—are the most important thing.

The problem with the mentality outlined above is that it is inwardly focused and stops you from seeing the situation objectively. By focusing on your feelings and responses, you will not be able to create a genuine connection with your interviewer. The attitude you should be cultivating leading up to your interview is, *"What can I do for this person?"* Ask yourself that over and over again, and what will happen is your focus will shift away from yourself to them, taking away any feelings of anxiety or fear that arise from self-focused thoughts.

Being a little nervous before an interview can be a good thing, as it keeps your mind and body sharp, alert and ready to respond. However, anything more that can hinder you from properly engaging with your interviewer and getting the most out of your time together. I'm sure you have either said or heard someone say, when asked how an interview went, "Ok I guess. It was a bit of blur". I interpret this as they weren't present nor fully engaged with their interviewer, dramatically reducing their likelihood for being a successful candidate.

When you shift your focus to the person sitting across from you, not to yourself or your performance, you will start to pick up their body language, facial expressions and tone of voice. When you respond to these and alter your behavior accordingly, the conversation will flow so much better and your interview will go from average to being a stand-out.

An example of this was my most recent interview, a month ago at the time of this writing. I had the privilege of already having a relationship with my interviewer, which also left me wide open as she already knew how I operated. Near the end she brought up a situation where she had asked something of me and I had never responded nor gave her what she needed. In my head I was scrambling for an answer knowing that there were a few reasons why I didn't help. I started to tell her that that particular week I had to step in for a colleague who was on leave and so I had to pick the most urgent tasks. As I was saying this, I could see her shuffling around in her chair, her eyes narrowing and her general expression telling me she did not like this answer. Immediately I course-corrected and took ownership of it, turning it into an opportunity for improvement; that I needed to communicate my priorities better. She softened instantly, and moved on.

In the end I did get the job and as for that particular task, she had already understood why I couldn't do it but wanted to see what my response would be. The moral of this story is that it doesn't matter how right you are in a situation, all that matters in that room is how you are perceived. She wanted to see that I was self-aware enough to recognise my weaknesses and own it.

You need to be clear and present, taking in every signal from your interviewer, absorbing everything they say, being authentic in your conversation and above all, demonstrating that you are someone who is teachable and reliable.

Self-awareness allows you to self-correct

If it helps, make a list of things that you bring to the role and ways that you can solve problems for this team. I guarantee, if you bring this list up during your interview, your interviewer will struggle to forget you. This is another application of serving people and is a theme you will see popping up in the book over and over again.

Because this book is aimed for graduates, I wanted to make this last point quite clear. When I went through the program, it was all about me, my development, my career, and my goals. Going into my rotations, it was the manager who had to fill out what they would get "their grad" working on and the skills they would develop. We actually had a joke in my first rotation that the instruction list for my manager was so long he felt like he had just ordered a flower in a flowerpot who needed constant watering, attention, and care, i.e. keep your grad happy, busy, and make sure your grad is getting the best experience. I agree this is necessary, due to some managers taking the system for granted and paying zero attention to career development. However, for many, this cultivated a "me-focused" attitude within myself over that first year. When I went for my first permanent role, I admit I did have a sense of entitlement over the 20 or so external applicants. Looking back, this was a terrible way to approach the interview, and had I realized this within myself, I would have changed it.

When you ask yourself, "What can I do for them?" the next logical question would be, "Who are they?" Find out who is conducting your interview and have a quick online gander, using the below as a starting point:

- Have they posted articles or blogs?
- How long have they been in their current role?
- What do they usually repost, i.e. what topics are they passionate about?
- Do you have any mutual connections?

If you work towards having them become a person in your mind and not a vehicle through which you can land a role, the rest of it should come pretty easily. Jot down ways that you can incorporate this into the conversation, knowing full well that almost all interviewers will leave a few minutes at the end for you to ask questions. This brings me to the next stage, the questions at the end, probably one of the most underestimated and underused portions of the interview.

Many people see the Q&A at the end as a time to ask further questions about the role. The worst response I've seen is, "So what will I be working on?" This is not the time nor place to have such discussions and, for me, was an immediate turn-off no matter how well the interview had gone up to that point, as it is inwardly focused and forces the interviewer into a corner. I believe this is where you can turn your interview from average to memorable. Take the information you have gathered about the team, the company, the financials, and the interviewer themselves and formulate some insightful and unique questions that shows your passion and seriousness about the position. I personally hate fluffy books that don't give you what you need to make this practical, so here are some I've used in the past and examples from the best interviews I've seen.

About the role

Can you tell me more about why you chose A over B to focus on in your strategy this year?

This shows that you have taken the time to find the strategy and have applied your own understanding to it. By asking a probing question, you are showing that you don't just accept things because they are there, but you use your experience and knowledge to try to improve it. The caveat here is that you don't assume to know best or ask this in an arrogant way. Use a soft tone of voice and be keen to learn.

What do you enjoy most about your team?

This will reveal to you what your future manager or peers enjoy doing, and the culture. They could jokingly answer "Friday drinks", which implies a relaxed social environment, or "testing new technologies or ways of working", which implies openness to a different way of doing things. They could also say "the high-pressure environment", which will tell you early on the expectations of you in the role.

What is the biggest myth about working in this team, industry, company?

I really like this one, as it makes them think creatively about their role and shows that them that you are not only considering the job, but the industry as a whole and the wider company. This goes back to the "executive mind" section in "Serve".

About them

How do you define success in your life?

Not everyone defines success as a certain pay grade or title. The answer to this will allow you greater insight into what is important to your manager, and you can then tailor your conversations to that (see "Advanced Networking").

If you could do a TED talk on a topic, what would it be?

Again, a quick way to find out what their passions are, very possibly external to their role.

What advice would you give your 20- to 25-year-old self?

Hint: take it onboard.

* Disclaimer: Please don't use more than two of these suggestions; it is not a rapid-fire session.

With this mental shift in mind, you are now positioned well to walk into that interview knowing that you've stacked the odds in your favour. You are no longer nervous, because it is not about you anymore, it is about them and their team.

When you apply for a role, chances are you are not just applying for one but have a few in mind. I had about three preferences that were all decent opportunities, but naturally I favoured one over the other two. The worst thing you can do here is to give off the impression to your interviewer that this role isn't your first preference.

You may think this is obvious, but I've been in interviews where the graduates didn't explicitly state this, yet their attitude and posture told us otherwise. It didn't matter how well they answered the questions or told us what we wanted to hear; the hunch that we were not their first choice was enough to cross them off the list. You need to convince each interviewer that the role you are discussing is all you want, and you will do anything it takes to be successful in it.

A technique you can use to achieve this is by taking notes. I'm not a fan of note taking on a tablet or phone, either; I'm talking about old-school, notebook-and-pen note taking, so the other person can see you writing. When I've written down what my interviewer is saying about the role, or the team or anything of interest, they immediately notice and give me more information. This is because you are making them feel heard, are engaged fully, and are valuing their precious time. When you show a keenness to learn, they will usually offer up more to you, which may be the difference in you getting the role over someone else with similar qualifications. So, whether you are in an interview, a mentoring session, or just a catch-up with someone in your network, make sure you use this technique to make the most out of your time and theirs.

REAL LIFE
IS NOT LIKE
UNIVERSITY;
YOUR
SCORE
IS NOT THE
GOVERNING
FACTOR TO
SUCCESS

04

Personal Branding

While I write this book, the company I work for is going through one of the biggest restructures in over a decade. By the end of it, almost every team will have been affected in some way, leaving everyone questioning their current contribution and reputation. The realization that you are not entitled to your position, but that it constantly needs to be earned was profound for me. I had to literally *graduate* from the graduate mentality of entitlement and understand that you need to be always working on yourself and your career. Never have I seen the power of a strong personal brand more than I have now, as it has been the difference between having high amounts of anxiety over losing your role and confidence that no matter what the outcome, you will find your way.

The beauty about being outside the graduate program is that I can see different ways people apply the idea of personal branding to their careers. I've seen some do it through showing up at every work event possible and plastering it on social media or LinkedIn and tagging everyone they can, trying to have coffee with everyone they meet, putting all their energy into dressing a certain way, or a combination of all three. By the way, I'm not against any of these strategies and I sometimes use them myself, but what is lacking is how to use them wisely so that people don't perceive you as inauthentic or fake.

The goal of your brand is trust.

Take a quick look at the brands that you buy from the most and ask yourself, why is it that you choose them over others time and time again? For me, it rarely has anything to do with it being a better product, but because they have sold me on the idea that they care about my frustrations and pains more than anyone else. I honestly don't place much emphasis on who has the most powerful colour palette or memorable slogans, but on whose service makes me feel like I am their sole priority. Branding yourself is no different.

No matter how senior someone is or how logical they seem, everyone has an emotional side where there is a drive for connection and purpose in everything they do. The reason having a strong personal brand is so powerful is that it taps into this emotional side and can help you land roles, create unity within your team, or simply make others want to help you when they don't have to. These things are essential to having a successful career where people want to work with you and for you.

Because your personal brand is exactly that, personal, i.e. *you*, without realising it we have been addressing this topic throughout the entire book! When you understand that the seemingly mundane or low-priority work you are doing is actually a shortcut to hone your leadership abilities, you will quickly develop a reputation for being someone that does not consider any work as being beneath them. This is critical to developing trust as opposed to being perceived as flighty and uncommitted.

These attributes are always obvious during interviews where managers are looking for candidates who they can trust, because they will consistently perform without having shiny ball syndrome.

The types of examples they use to answer questions can make this really clear to potential managers. For example, when graduates have talked about how they were able to present a new strategy, own relationships with customers or be solely responsible for moving project x forward, I cannot help but think "how will this person perform when their work isn't so exciting or when they are not in front of executives?". Don't get me wrong, these are incredible opportunities to be having and I most certainly had these however, be aware that managers are seldom impressed by flashy examples. Really good managers want to see you getting your hands dirty and being ok with supporting them and their team, no matter how that looks.

Pick and choose what experiences you share so that you cultivate your reputation as someone who is willing to be teachable and open to contributing in the way that is needed. This is central to developing your brand, and will give you great leverage as you start to advance in your career.

When you focus on creating real and authentic two-way relationships with people in your network, you will be seen as trustworthy of people's time and effort. All it takes is one good contact to vet you to someone in *their* network and you will never have a shortage of opportunities or people to count on when you need them.

Combine these with the next chapter on clarity and you will have an unshakeable foundation upon which people can trust you with their vision, time, and money. Now that we have the fundamentals out of the way, we can focus on the fun stuff, the things that I found were the icing on my branding cake.

Here is the list of things that I did outside of working hours during my first 18 months:

- Published 6 blogs
- Published 3 articles
- Featured on 4 panels
- Moderated 3 panels
- Spoke to audiences of 200+
- Filmed two tours of the company facilities
- Photographed for graduate campaigns
- Won an industry award
- Wrote 10-15 LinkedIn posts on events I hosted or contributed to

Some of you could be reading this thinking you've done a lot more or some of you could be overwhelmed and didn't realise these things were important. This list has nothing to do with me showing off; in fact, sometimes I think I didn't take advantage of more opportunities that came up! I want to show you this so you can start thinking about different ways to add to your *portfolio of life.*

Part of one of my roles during the program was to help organise hackathons that were held over the weekends, to learn how they run and how we can use some of these principles in a large company. One weekend, as I was sitting around fairly bored and waiting for the teams to finish the first stage of their "start-up", I started to chat with one of the ladies who was organising the event. She began talking about how people today change careers much more rapidly than they did thirty years ago, and events like this show that people want to get involved with things unrelated to their jobs. Many of the hackathon participants were lawyers, accountants, or managers who had a passion for creating and executing new solutions, which is what brought them along to the event that weekend. As I started to talk about some projects I was also involved in, she mentioned that younger people will not only change careers but seek ways to add to their portfolio of life. That beautiful phrase struck me hard. I viewed my work as being my work, and my side projects as being separate. Thinking of all these things as one portfolio of my life changed the way I saw my personal brand.

Let me expand on this a little further. During my first year, I tended to get ultra-focused on making sure I was performing to a high standard for my manager, and if someone offered me to be involved with something external to that, I usually rejected it or made sure my team knew about it so it would add to my performance review. I didn't understand how branding worked, nor how you can do small things now that will set you up for bigger opportunities further down the track. Once I caught this idea of all the activities during my week as adding to the broader story and toolkit of my life, I started getting intentional.

I love writing. I've always journaled since I was in high school and enjoy reading back over the last ten years of my life like a book with many chapters. Even though I was working within a technical stream, I gravitated to being the one to write up the reports or summarising what we'd worked on. It never occurred to me that I could use it to create a professional voice for myself and stand out amongst my peers. I have to give full credit of this to my manager, Frank, for making blogs one of my KPIs. When my team created a software bot that could automate certain tasks, my job was to write and post a blog about it. Sounds simple, but the thought was terrifying. Why would people care about my thoughts? What if someone tears apart my analysis or technical points? What will my fellow graduates think of me? Am I trying to hard?

I put it off for a month out of the fear that it was not perfect enough and that Frank might forget about it. He didn't, and I finally posted it on LinkedIn and opened myself up to the judgements of the world. It felt huge and I didn't go online to check it for weeks.

When I did, I saw that it had reached thousands of viewers and the comments were generally positive! People were supportive and loved the way it was easy to understand and that it came from someone just starting out. I got addicted to that feeling and wrote my next blog not long after. This is where life rewards you for taking action. I received an email from our branding team, who had noticed I was taking initiative to grow my reputation and doing something a little different. They asked me to be part of their graduate campaign for the following year and wanted me to write about my career so far. I was shocked. There was a photoshoot that went along with the story, which was used all over the country. It was an exciting time, and it never got old bumping into my face in magazines, websites, and events!

Things naturally progressed from there when I took the time to develop those new relationships with people from branding, communications, HR, and marketing. It was a side of the business I had never been exposed to, and I wanted to take advantage of it. That resulted in me being involved with filmed tours, other career blogs, events, panels, and interviews.

I wanted to give you these details of my journey because I want you to see that so much of this part of your career you cannot plan; rather, it comes as a result of you taking action. What can you do now that is unique to you and gives you a voice? That could be doing what I did and writing a blog, putting your hand up to be involved with the next cohort of graduates, offer mentoring if that comes naturally to you, or setting up a networking group of grads across different companies so you broaden your career outlook!

The moral of this story is to not rely on your program or company to give you these opportunities; you must go out and create them. Remember that every tool or skill, writing, public speaking, hosting, mentoring, etc., that you learn on the way will be added to your resume, making you a formidable candidate for any role you desire.

VISION HE WITH THE CLEAREST LEADS

05

Clarity Is Power

Change of pace. I believe by now you have created a key list of people within your network, are actively growing your relationships with them, and have a balanced view about the roles you are interested in. These things alone will create so much stability on your journey and hopefully get you where you want to be faster! Assuming you know where it is you want to get to, which leads me perfectly to our next topic, goal setting. Feel free to read through this first and come back later to work through the process, as it will take some time and energy to complete properly.

This is not a chapter that will go through the SMART method, which stands for Specific, Measurable, Achievable, Relevant, and Time-bound. The job of Google is to give you strategies for the masses, but I believe this is just one piece of the puzzle, and to get a better picture, we need to go deeper in order for you to strive towards something inspiring that you will carry with you your whole life and will be your true north. I want to start by sharing my experience with the conventional way of setting goals.

Most graduate programs have development days where you learn skills and processes to help you succeed in your work. In one of these sessions, we had to set some goals for our careers. The method was to come up with three or four goals that you wanted to achieve in the next few years and then break them down into actionable steps that you could do now. There was nothing wrong with this other than I had no idea what to write as my goals! Why would I? Up to this point, my only goals had been achieving the score I needed to get into my course, passing all my exams, applying for jobs and programs, and now finally I am where I want to be. I had never given thought to where to go from here.

Some of you may already have a clear idea of where you want to go in your career and that's wonderful; you can work at refining that by using some of the tactics in "Networking". But how about in your wealth, health, or relationships? Chances are, you have goals in one or some of these areas but not all, and in the spirit of creating a resource for you to achieve success, we cannot avoid discussing these other areas that also make up your life.

The one with the clearest vision leads.

We all are attracted to people who know where they are going, whether it be in work, in health, in business, or even in family. Personally, my social media feed is full of people that I want to emulate in order to bring more success into my life. Why? Because they have a voice, they have direction, and they have results.

If you do not have a vision for your life, rest assured someone else will and you will live the kind of life that is bombarded with other people's opinions and priorities, leaving you ultimately struggling to take control. I've seen this happen on smaller scales around holiday or wedding planning, and large ones which can determine someone's career path or future. Get clear on your life, and you will very quickly be able to lead others with conviction and magnetism.

Before we get stuck into this, I want to do a little bit of mental housekeeping to make sure we are starting off on a solid foundation about why this is important to do.

Let's start with energy. As you move further into your career, energy becomes the second most important asset behind time. In my own life, I've seen that I have less energy for things I used to do around friendships, events, reading, or even energy to focus on my health and exercise. Much of my energy got consumed by work, the new relationships I needed to develop within my network, and events that would grow my branding. Because I wasn't focused on anything in particular, time flew by and before I knew it, I had been working for a year and had no recollection of all the things I had achieved. Not defining my goals and creating a plan for my time and energy was a risk I couldn't afford any longer.

If you cannot measure it, you cannot grow it.

Taking the time to set effective goals and a plan to achieve them is imperative if you want to move forward in all areas of life with limited time and energy.

The second thing is gratitude. Before you can begin to set any goals, you need to be appreciative of the things that are currently in your life. If you cannot do this on a regular basis, you will find it very difficult to achieve your goals, as you are setting them from a place of scarcity and desperation. I've noticed that when this happens, I struggle to set goals that inspire me to work to a higher standard because I am focused on the lack in my life.

So, before you shoot for the stars, write a list of everything you are grateful for in your health, wealth, and relationships. For me, it was simple, as I had no terminal illnesses, had enough money and income to buy what I needed, and had a supportive family and partner. These are the basics from which you can start, and I encourage you to get hyper specific on the things that you are really grateful for. When you get going on this, you will notice a positive change toward your outlook on life. Every time I go through this, I feel much more energized and inspired to be a better person and grow these areas further. What you have done is change your state.

Your state is one of the most important things you control in your life, and accessing your peak state is one of the most effective ways to draw out your passions and desires, which can be used to create inspiring goals that propel you forward.

You know the saying, "What happens to you is 10% and how you respond is 90%"? Well, this is the key. We've all seen our favorite sports people do this, whether it's the rigorous routine of tennis players before a match to achieve the ultimate mental state to win, or the loud, pumping music at a boxing match to create adrenaline within the fighters. State has a huge part to play in outcomes, and you are no different. Writing a list of what you are grateful for is a powerful way to access this state. Additional ways could be going for a run to get those endorphins going, playing music that creates positive energy within you, sitting in a particular way, wearing particular clothes, or anything that makes you feel like you're in control and on top of things. Now you are in a prime position to start jotting down some key phrases, words, or ideas of the person that you want to be in all areas of your life.

*the DNA of the oak tree already
exists within the acorn*

One of my favorite phrases is that the *DNA of the oak tree already exists within the acorn.* In other words, the person you are destined to become already lies within you and it is your job to pull it out, define it, and create a plan to execute it. That is what goal setting is in its purest form. I have read and been to countless talks on goal setting and very rarely do people acknowledge that, for goals to be really achievable, you need to be inspired by them. And for you to be inspired, they need to come from a place inside you that speaks to the core of who you are.

So, let's make this simple. Below your gratitude list, write out the top 10-20

- things you want to be in your life that you've never been
- things you want to do that you've never done
- things you want to experience that you've never experienced
- things you want to learn that you've never learnt
- things you want to see that you've never seen

Getting more than five things out for some of these was hard for me initially, so come back to it if you need time to think or relax. When you start asking these questions, your brain will begin trying to find answers during the day and you may surprise yourself what comes to the surface! The key with this is to be completely honest with yourself and not to impose onto it what you *think* you should write. Then take each of these lists and cut them down to the top five (or even better, three) by comparing them and deciding which ones get you the most excited. Once you have this handful of things that you want to be, do, experience, learn, and see, you can begin to create goals that speak to the essence of who you are through your increased self-awareness.

The advantages of knowing what your core values are goes well beyond work and can have a big role to play in how successful your relationships are. If you are dating someone who values their alone time above all else, and your value is spending time together, you have a recipe for conflict. Having a clear understanding of your own values can help you find the right type of friend or partner where you are not always in conflict trying to change their values to match your own.

Although these are not specific career goals, they will help you when you need to make decisions around future roles, companies, or even countries! Getting these life goals out on paper gives you a solid foundation upon which to build your health, wealth, career, and relationship goals, as you now know what you really value.

To get you started on these specific goals, I've found answering the *what, who, how, why* is the most thorough way to get everything out. You can then refine it back as you get clearer on what you want to achieve in that area.

Write down as much as you can around:

- *What do you want to be or achieve in relation to your health, wealth, career, and relationships?*
- *Who does it relate to? Are you doing it to, with, or for them?*
- *How will you do this? What daily or weekly actions will you take consistently to see this through?*
- *Why do you want it? (Having a good answer to this will help you when you want to give up.)*

While you are in this head space, there is one myth I would like to bust, and that is the "passion" myth. I went through a period of disillusionment within my first 18 months, as all the areas I wanted to work in and the skills I wanted to develop never got me that excited. I started to get worried because people always talked about being passionate about what you do, but nothing I came across made me feel that way. I'm sure you've heard, "Do what you love and you'll never work a day in your life." I began to panic wondering how I was meant to be passionate about something that I didn't love, or what did loving your job actually mean?

These thoughts were always at the back of my mind until I came across an article that talked about how you *develop* passion. This flipped everything on its head, as I always thought that when you found the right role, you knew it was right because you were passionate about it. This thinking places a huge amount of pressure on everything you do and creates an unrealistic expectation with a career that could be pure fantasy. As a result, you use up so much energy and time trying to find that perfect role that fits what you think it should be!

Passion is developed when you master something.

I encourage you to test this and speak to people in your life whom you know are passionate about something. I have people in my team who actually love what they do and go above and beyond because they are passionate. It wasn't the passion that came first, but they worked to become knowledgeable in that area and now enjoy having influence and making decisions that create change. They have mastered something and as a result, have a passion for it. Don't be afraid if you don't love what you are doing straight away; it doesn't matter.

The right question to ask yourself is, "Do I like it enough or am I curious enough to stick with it and master it?" If yes, commit to learning and giving it your best shot, and watch how passion can develop to the point where you are genuinely grateful and enjoy what you do.

There is one final thought I want to leave you with around goal setting and clarity. I mentioned earlier that much of your purpose in life already exists within you, and it is your job to pull it out, define it, and take action on it. I encourage you to make a new tab on whatever note-taking software or notebook you have and write down every time you do something that makes you feel alive or most like yourself. Some of the notes I have written down have even been when someone else has said something about me that was one of the goals I had! I have found that the more of these I write down, the clearer it becomes what I want to do more of, like writing and inspiring people. If you make it a habit to record these moments, over time you will see a pattern emerging, which you can use as your true north for when life throws hurdles at you and you must make decisions around your health, wealth, career, and relationships.

So get clear, answer all these questions for yourself, and feel free to update them as your perspective expands and evolves. If you have a goal that you didn't reach, don't just label yourself a failure but find out what it was that stopped you. It could be people's opinions, your own limiting beliefs, past "failures", or just that it was harder work than you accounted for. Make sure you know what it was that stopped you, so you don't sabotage future goals. If the price was too high, that's okay, as it means you value something else more! Acknowledge it and re-adjust so that it continues to inspire you.

ACTION
TRUMPS
KNOWLEDGE
EVERYTIME

06

Gain It All, Keep It All

My biggest desire for you is to become successful. Because of this, I cannot end this book without acknowledging other areas of your life that can easily make or break you. Most of us are early on in the journey, and so I feel there is no better time than now to get your awareness cranking of how harnessing these areas can push you, or indeed pull you away from success.

These areas have the most impact on your life, and if one gets neglected, everything you have worked for can become jeopardized. I was very fortunate to have learned this from various teachers and want to provide a few learnings to each area that I believe can make a massive difference to your success at work.

At the end of each section, I have included an action list for you to implement right away.

My favourite quote from Tony Robbins is that;

knowledge is not power, it's potential power. If it was, we would all be billionaires with six-packs. Instead, action trumps knowledge every time. Small actions executed consistently will be what changes your life.

Let's start with health

How many successful businessmen do you know who have managed to create great wealth for themselves and their families but failed to maintain their own health, resulting in heart attacks, strokes, or diabetes later in life? Some of the language I've heard is that this is almost a token badge to success, putting your health at risk for the sake of your business. I've heard countless mentions of "I'm so run down", "I haven't slept in weeks", "my blood pressure is too high", and the old faithful "stressed out". But rarely do I see something being done about it until more severe symptoms present themselves.

This doesn't exist only at work but in student life. For me, that period was disastrous to my health, and I'm annoyed at myself for what I put my body through for the sake of cramming insane amounts of information into my brain for months at a time, culminating in a bender the weeks leading up to exams. My daily diet consisted of a sugar-laden chai on my commute in, a ham and cheese toastie for my first lecture, fried chicken for lunch (maybe a ramen if I was feeling super healthy), a couple of donuts or chips for an afternoon study snack, and another chai on the way home. Then dinner was just whatever I could get my hands on while trying to get assignments done. Then there were the morning, midday, and afternoon "sessions" that ran my alcohol count through the roof. Drinking was a natural part of college life and gave me some of the best memories I have, but when it's almost triple the standard for most people, you have to take a good look at your habits.

Things got quite bad halfway through my degree when I woke up one night feeling nauseous, foggy, and disgusting after downing two or three packets of frozen lasagna (no, I'm not Garfield) and was incredibly thirsty, as I was always dehydrated. I knew this was a ticking time bomb and decided that night I would try an experiment on myself. For the rest of that semester, I cut one bad habit at a time, and ate fish as often as possible and healthier snacks, like bruschetta or oats. I swapped out the sugar chai for a black coffee or tea and kept a water bottle on me at all times. When we went out, I would swap out beer for a G&T or another spirit. I then supplemented with getting into the gym and training with weights, if only to manage my stress and taking out my frustration with assignments during the session. Within a few months, my grades had skyrocketed, and I was putting in less energy and retaining more. The funny thing was, the food swaps didn't make much of a difference to me; I didn't feel like I was missing out or craving the old stuff. That was the biggest surprise. It was a pretty simple experiment, and the results shouldn't come as a shock to anyone reading this. This was such a valuable lesson to me, and something that I have carried with me in my working life as well.

I was hesitant to share this, as society tends to go to extremes, especially with health, and what should be very simple can end up getting scarily complicated the more Netflix documentaries we watch. For me, it was as simple as reducing alcohol dramatically, drinking more water, watching my caffeine intake and swapping coffee for tea as often as possible, eating real food, and training. I had clarity of thinking and I could solve problems so much faster, read and absorb more, focus for longer periods, and not succumb to stress or anxiety as often.

I really wanted to include my story into this, as the first few months of the grad program were exactly like those days. You are meeting new and like-minded people, and socializing is a priority and you have the money for it. I slipped back into those habits pretty quickly, purely to the availability of it all. All I ask is that you remember that your performance can be impacted by your health, maybe not today, but in 10-20 years' time. If you don't believe me, you really don't have to look too far to see executives who look like they've lost control of their health habits and end up losing precious career time taking leave to manage it. Don't leave it until you have a family of your own and your career is advancing to deal with it, as you will have more of a correction to make with less time.

I've summarized some additional things that have helped me remain focused and alert, allowing me to take on more at work without the stress that comes with it.

Actions to take

⌐ Start your morning with a lemon water: rather than dehydrate your body first thing in the morning with caffeine, hydrate it and set it up to absorb more nutrients throughout the day.

⌐ Cut back your coffees. If you do a lot of office catch-ups, order a tea, matcha, or turmeric latte. Have a "latte limit" in mind that works for you.

⌐ Bring snacks with you like nuts, dried fruit, protein shakes, or protein balls. I found that I bought the worst lunches when I was famished.

⌐ As soon as you can, take on a weekly or bi-weekly resistance training routine. Getting the help of a personal trainer is a great way to start. The more muscle you have, the more efficient your body is at burning calories and fat and providing you with far more energy. This will also come in super handy during flu season, as your immune system will be strong.

Now, wealth

I wanted to share some simple principles that have helped me tremendously and have gotten me to a position where I am planning to not be dependent on "active" income much earlier than the current 65-year-old average.

Let's start with the 10/10/20 rule.

This rule states that if you save 10% of your income, invest it into something that yields a 10% average annual return, you can have full income replacement in 20 years. This is the power of compounding, and if you increase the savings percentage just by a fraction, you can bring this down even more.

I am a huge fan of timeless classics containing wisdom to last centuries and hold true through different economic seasons. This is because my wealth game is too important to leave to chance or bank it all on the latest investment craze. I believe if it was written 100 years ago and was successful to people then, it will be successful to people now and 100 years from now. The two books I began this journey with are:

⌐ Think & Grow Rich (written in 1937)
⌐ The Richest Man in Babylon (written in 1926)

Almost everything written today on wealth building has its roots in one or both of these books. Start with these and you will have a foundation that most people do not. If you listen to interviews with Warren Buffett, Ray Dalio, Tony Robbins, Rob Icahn, etc., they will all give this advice that is found in those books:

"save & invest"

It sounds hideously simple and almost like they are brushing off the question, but when I went back to basics and read those two books and other more recent ones, it became painfully obvious that this truth was all I needed to focus on to create a life where I won't have to worry about finances. Now let's make it practical.

Save. save. save. This should not even be a decision that you need to make each time you receive your salary. If you are not already saving 10% of your income, put this book down and get onto your online bank account and set up an automated savings transfer each fortnight or month. Calculate what 10% is and make sure that every pay cycle, that money goes into your savings account. This is not rocket science, and if anyone has read any modern bestsellers like Rich Dad Poor Dad, Money: Master the Game, or The Barefoot Investor, this will be a trivial part of this book. This sounds harsh, but if you don't do this, don't bother spending more time figuring out how to build wealth. If the advice of the most successful investors and richest people on earth isn't good enough, nothing will be. I know savings doesn't sound sexy, but do you know what is? Being able to retire while all your colleagues are worrying over the next job, or how they will support their lifestyle if they couldn't work anymore for whatever reason. This thought was enough for me to boost my savings percentage by 2-3% each quarter as I managed my expenses better.

One other thing to keep in mind, this rule holds true whether you are earning $1000 or $100,000 each week. If this is not a habit today, it won't be when you are earning a higher income. It took me a while to get into the habit of saving because I thought that it would be easier when I got the next increase or new role, but I knew when that day came, I would value my lifestyle over saving and just make it harder for myself to create this habit. This applies to all income, including side hustles, start-ups, or bonuses.

10% should be the bare minimum, and if you cannot manage this, you need to take a good look at your expenses and see where you can source this from. When this becomes routine, you will be surprised at how quickly you get used to living on slightly less. Tweak and grow this each quarter to accelerate your wealth growth.

Second is to invest. This is where a book like *Money* by Tony Robbins can come in handy, guiding you step by step on how to create a simple portfolio to achieve this based on what the most successful investors on earth are doing. I'm not a licensed financial advisor but something to keep in mind is that the S&P 500 index has returned 9.5% on average since conception in 1928. An index fund like this means you are buying into the brightest minds and most profitable companies on earth rather than trying to pick the next Microsoft or Apple. Passive investing, or long-term investing, doesn't have to be complicated or difficult. Spend some time reading up on this and ways to create a diverse portfolio, which you can set up in less than a couple of hours.

If you want to go old school and read from the father of long-term investing himself, Benjamin Graham, who was Warren Buffets mentor, pick up *The Intelligent Investor* and take your time going through it and understand what he is saying. After I put this book down, I had so much clarity over how I should structure my investments and understood the pulse of the market so much better. This confidence is what will keep you stableduring periods where you are struggling to save or not seeing results fast enough. He has a famous mantra, which is usually never far from my mind:

Buy your stocks like groceries, not like perfume.

This simply means that you should use the money you have saved to invest in your portfolio of stocks at regular intervals, just as you would regularly buy groceries. This makes full use of time diversification and allows you to approximate the market mean, which for me is every quarter.

So, there it is. Save and invest. This is the foundation to the 10/10/20 rule, putting you on track to becoming less dependent on active income but slowly replacing it with passive income so that you have the freedom to do the things you want to do.

The second timeless wealth principle that you will hear or read in many places is to serve people. In fact, that is all businesses are! They create products or services that serve people and alleviate problems in exchange for money. This is why I chose to start this book off with the "Serve" chapter, as it is a fundamental attitude you need in order to be successful, whether it is working for someone else or for yourself. It all comes down to how well you can serve people, whether your boss, your team, or your clients.

Solve a problem and you will create value. Create value and you will create wealth.

Actions to take

⌐ Read Think & Grow Rich and The Richest Man in Babylon
   Set up an automated savings account

⌐ Learn about time diversification

⌐ Research the history of the stock market and the S&P 500
   index

⌐ Leverage books like Money: Master the Game to learn how
   the greats have their portfolios set up

⌐ Every 3-6 months, take your savings and put it into your
   investment portfolio

Now that we have discussed health and wealth, I want to briefly touch on the other areas that make up the entirety of your life. There are many different versions of this floating around and I want you to choose one that resonates with you the most, but within my own life I have noted the following areas are the most relevant:

- Health
- Wealth
- Relationships
- Career/Business
- Recreation
- Personal Growth
- Spirituality

I tend to visualise these areas as individual spokes of a wheel that contribute to my overall journey forward.

If one or more of these areas gets neglected, the wheel becomes weakened and ceases to be able to do its job properly, if not stopping me completely.

A great habit to get into is to constantly assess where you are in each of these areas and where your energy and attention needs to be directed to. For example, every 3-6 months, I sit down and answer a series of questions about each area that allow me to rank them from 1-10. From there, I can quickly see if my life is out of balance and where I need to put in more effort.

This can then feed back into your goals or your overall life strategy, allowing you to move forward with clarity, knowing that you will not burn out due to your improved self-awareness.

Sometimes thinking about these areas as a whole can be quite daunting, and I find the easiest way to keep moving forward is to do something small every day. Being consistent with the small things over the weeks and months will turn into a massive difference that can change your life.

if you do what you've always done, you'll get what you've always gotten

Quick wins to improve each area of your wheel

Health: Prioritise 7-8 hours of sleep each night and keep hydrated. Water is the ultimate detoxifier, keeping your mind and body functioning optimally.

Wealth: Think of how you can "reduce and transfer" an expense this week. For example, rather than just thinking you will cut a coffee or two this week, think about it as though the $4-10 saved through your reduction of coffee will be transferred into your investments, contributing to your freedom later in life. This is a much more positive way to think about expense control.

Relationships: Take the time to thank a mentor, friend, or family member for something specific they have taught you. This overlooked action will immediately strengthen your relationship with them.

Career/Business: Dedicate 30 minutes to learn/develop a new skill, i.e. Google/Facebook Ads, coding language, speed reading, CPR, tactics to remembering people's names, etc. Anything that can give you an edge.

Recreation: Keep this time separate from everything else. It is so easy to have your emails or messages notifying you when you are attempting to relax or enjoy your hobby. This defeats the whole purpose, so switch off completely when you are setting time aside to rest and recharge.

Personal Growth: Read for 1 hour or get an audible subscription, in which case you can listen while in the car or cleaning your house.

Spirituality: Thinking back to the goal setting chapter, create a tab or section wherever you take your notes and make a point to write down all the moments that you felt you were truly doing what you love. For me, it was the times I was writing or talking about this book! Don't lock it down to work or business, but even when you are relaxing or being with people. When you build up a list, you will find those patterns that will enable you to understand what makes you tick.

STANDING ON THE SHOULDERS OF GIANTS

07

Let's Ask the Boss

When I began putting this book together, my number one priority was to give as many ideas and principles to you as I could in the hopes that some of these will stick and enable you to get to where you want to go. So far, these principles have been from my perspective, and although I have used timeless strategies and ideas, I wanted to make sure you had an even wider scope of advice.

So, I've put together an interview-style chapter for you where I have reached out to leaders and managers from within my personal network to find out their thoughts and experiences with graduates. Many of them have been through internships or graduate programs themselves and are still heavily involved with them, and therefore understand where you are at.

In order to keep things flowing, I've included each of their answers beneath each question, so you can soak it all up rather than going back and forth through each interview. If you would like more information about these individuals, reach out to me via the link at the back of this book and I will endeavour to help where I can. I learnt a lot speaking with them and I hope you will too!

What is your definition of success?

Name: Kath
Position: Partner
Career length: 23 years

Kath: To raise happy, responsible, and compassionate people who give back rather than take. When I look back at my life, I was all take take take. Now, I want to leave a legacy where I've made an impact and difference. It's not about making money but helping people and growing things. I am curious about life, and my career has reflected that. I am always trying to figure out what can we do better, and answering that question for people. My time is valuable, so I want to spend my time how I can spend it. If I can optimise something, I will. I do not like to waste time.

Name: Jass
Position: Sales
Career length: 5 years

Jass: It comes down to the individual. Success is different for everyone. Some people want relationships, wealth, career progression—define it for yourself and then work to achieve what that looks like. For me, it's having a good work environment, money, career progression, and seeing younger people I've mentored do well.

Name: Louisa
Position: Industry influencer
Career length: 19 years

Louisa: Workplace and life are interlinked. I always ask myself "Am I learning from people around me and always growing in the work that I am doing?" Are you testing yourself and pushing yourself to achieve everything you can at that point in your life? Are you getting feedback from people around you? Feedback can come from managers, customers, or your boss, but you need that feedback to keep you on track. Personally, if you're happy at work and you are successful, that feeds into your happiness at home. I started my career in sales and so success was whether you made your number or not. As long as you tick that box, you feel successful. As a person, I've never been satisfied with that. It's been more fulfilling having great relationships with customers and knowing that they enjoy doing business with me. My personality cannot make success just about the number, but I want those additional factors such as respect, using things outside my job to learn new skills, and helping people. I'm not content with resting on the easiest measure of success.

Name: Chris
Position: Software Developer
Career length: 15 years

Chris: It's changed over the years. When I got my graduate role, it was about getting a good job, attaining the right certifications, chasing the latest technology. But now, later on, I focus heavily on learning something new every single time, whether that is a new framework, or technology stack. For me now, success is to allow myself to follow the evolution of trends and as long as I remain interested, then that is success. That's only the career aspect, but my family is also a part of what success means to me.

What is the biggest lesson you have learnt in your career so far?

Kath: I was raised to try to do my best. Don't do it half-assed, but do it to the best of your ability. The flowers in the field don't compete with each other, they just bloom and all are beautiful in their own right. You don't have to constantly look over your shoulder or try to out-do your peers. I don't do good work because there is a moral dessert at the end; rather, the reward is that I know I've done well. Integrity is your brand, so don't short-change yourself because people around you may be. I have found that there is a lot of people out there who do things half-assed, but you don't have to be the same.

Jass: How to delineate between personal and professional relationships. When you have a social relationship with someone, how does that impact your work life? Likewise, if you don't, how does that also impact you? Does that creep into how you operate at work? Do you give or withhold favour or preference? Treat everyone with an even hand regardless of how you are with them outside of work. You're not going to have social relationships with everyone but treat them all the same.

Louisa: There is this saying going around that you need to bring your whole self to work. I agree with this; however, there is an aspect where you need to be able to navigate the challenging situation, which is you are working every day for five days a week with people you may or may not choose as your friends. You need to find that blend of your authentic self but always being mindful of how you interact with others to bring out the best in them. Early on, I was really not myself, as I was guarded and felt I had to act a certain way. To fit in, I wore pantsuits because I didn't want to draw too much attention to myself. This same thought process is applicable to men too.

The flowers in the field don't compete with each other, they just bloom and all are beautiful in their own right

My husband hates wearing a tie, as it's uncomfortable and too formal. He has evolved his dress to suit him but still be appropriate for work.

Chris: Don't settle for just being comfortable. Everything has a rhythm and you get can used to it. When I find myself not learning something new but treading water, maintaining and not evolving, that is mundane, and I have to move to something else. I may not have anything left to give to my team. This happened to me coming straight out of my graduate role. I had various jobs that lasted 4 years, and after that I would feel the itch to try something new. You can have a different title but be doing essentially the same job, repeating yourself for years. That was the biggest wake-up call in my career. I would also say to attend more meet-ups with like-minded people. Attending those events allows you to meet people outside your job but who have a similar mindset to you. It offers a completely different perspective when you see how somebody else works. They could offer you something that you could never have stumbled upon yourself.

If you could give your 23-year-old self advice, what would it be?

Kath: I didn't take a job in Boston, and looking back, I should have taken it. There were reasons why I didn't at the time, but it was an opportunity I should have embraced. I would tell myself to not stay too long in a role or company if you know it's bad or draining you as a person. You know when it's not the thing you want to do. Find something else, because there is always another option. If you don't have the skills, learn them. Find something that gives you the passion and the drive to lift yourself out of your circumstances.

Jass: Be humbler and put yourself out there. Do tasks that are a bit crap, but in reality, know that it opens up doors. It's good to be confident but not arrogant. To make sure you are addressing this, try to be engaged in something you think is a waste of your time or a task that you'd not think is stimulating but in the end may get you some results. This could be going to more events, taking on more projects, getting to graduate panels, sharing your experiences. Make sure you get feedback constantly. If you disagree with it, it's okay, but understand what perception you have within an organization.

Louisa: This one can be hard to explain to someone in their early twenties, as it is almost too soon to work through it, but if you can, work out what your demons are professionally. I had a big problem with public speaking. Even when I was a little girl, I was too scared to answer the phone at home. That lead to a general fear of publicly expressing my voice. In my twenties, I didn't realise how deeply rooted it was. If I had unpacked that problem earlier, I know I would be more successful than I am now, because public speaking is such a critical piece of being seen as a leader. You need to speak with inspiration and authority. I look back and wish I had dealt with and recognised it sooner than bumbling through and thinking I would be fine. Be very pragmatic about what your weaknesses are and take steps to deal with them as soon as possible. That will take some self-reflection and not many people do that in their twenties. Don't let things get worse.

Chris: It comes back to learning. I studied geology and then was unsuccessful with getting a job in the industry. My heart wasn't in it, and on the side, I was learning computer science. I would say to keep following your interests and pick up those soft skills. Listen to what people are saying or feedback they are giving. You are surrounded by people whom have so much experience and you get to tap into that by just listening. What makes a product great? How do you build a great team? These are so much more important than just the textbook experience. Focus on those soft skills rather than putting yourself into a box because of your degree.

What is the worst advice you've heard given to graduates?

Kath: To dress a certain way or "tone yourself down" to emulate your colleagues. You spend 40 hours a week at work and if you don't have the freedom to be yourself, you will burn out.

Jass: Just network. People don't understand what that actually means. So many people organise coffee meetings that don't actually do anyone any good. Have they researched, understand the position the person is in, or even what their unit does? Make sure you do it with purpose. Have a plan of what you are going to get out of it, knowing that that person is taking time out of their day to meet with you.

Louisa: I will answer this one a little differently. It's not so much the actual advice given is sometimes bad, but it's how people give it. When people give advice, they generally have a wealth of experience, and so they will say something like,"I didn't have any qualifications, so you don't need this degree or that degree." They don't translate their experience into today's reality. That is when it's poor advice. When you give advice to grads, draw on your experience but recognise that directly advising them to do what you did may not be applicable. You need to intelligently translate it into how the world has changed or what part of that experience is relevant to the grads you are speaking to now. Don't assume they want to go on your exact same path. Rather than saying they do not need a degree, ask what has their degree done for them? For example, "Degrees are a great foundation, but what you are lacking is commercial experience." You are bringing it together in light of their experience and in a way that is relevant to them.

What are your general frustrations with graduates?

Jass: They sometimes have a sense of entitlement. Once you get the position, you can forget how hard it was to obtain it. They can sometimes expect the promotions, good work, and career progression to come naturally because they are on a graduate pathway. But during your time, you need to put in a lot of effort to earn that. I've seen many focus too much on networking whilst sacrificing upskilling themselves. Networking is only effective when paired with a good work ethic and initiative, knowing you have to put in long hours some nights. I also have frustrations with the "let me know" emails, let me know if I can help, let me know what I can do, etc. My advice is to do something, anything, that gets the ball rolling in a direction.

Louisa: I haven't had a huge amount of experience at working with them, but I think what I like to see are the basics. For instance, you come into a meeting and you have your notebook or iPad open and you are hungry to learn from what you are seeing. You are present and are taking in the learning opportunity. They can be a little too focused on the larger networking or career stuff, but you need to have the groundwork that comes with doing the menial tasks. I respect the grads who have asked me how this rotation serves their career aspiration, but you need to balance that with the willingness to see every opportunity you are given is an opportunity to learn, whether menial or sexy. If you are finding your tasks easy, put forward a proposal to automate something. You can inject some ideas of change to a manager who hasn't seen that yet. Have a bigger picture around your dream job as it might be a 15- or 20-year work in progress. I would encourage you to think about the small wins early in your career. I had shit sales accounts when I started, as they were not buying anything and the relationship was not good. I realised this was my chance to turn this around, and so over time I built that up and got them choosing us over competitors. I nailed the basics. I showed up and was reliable. Then I started reaping the rewards. You may have your head down for a couple of years before you start reaching more of your potential, but it's by getting the basics right that you grow and get more responsibility. Even people more senior don't get this. I have had people tell me they want to be a manager, and so when I go on leave I ask them to look after the team, and they are not prepared. There are stepping stones to everything you do, regardless of talent or connections. Those little stones will start to build momentum. When I wasn't enjoying my role for the first 5 years, I made sure those basics were nailed. When the rewards started to show, I realised how much I started to enjoy it. Sticking with it gave me the things I dreamt of when I was younger, which was financial security and working in Australia.

Chris: Some graduates I've had in my team have been very timid. If you're too shy to communicate or speak effectively, that is going to prohibit you and your career. You won't get the most out of your grad experience if these skills aren't learnt. I've been blessed with having motivated graduates, but there have been a few where I feel like they don't want to be here or that they're not interested. It makes you feel like you don't want to put any effort.

Do you have a story to share of when you met or had an ideal graduate? What did they do?

Kath: I do, and he was fearless. At the start, he was really soft spoken and unsure of himself, but he was very technically smart. I sat him down and told him to try everything, saying what was the worst that was going to happen? He is now an executive 10 years later, partly because he went out and tried things and ended up finding something that came very naturally to him. When he found it, I mentored him further in that direction. I don't think he would be at the level he is today if someone hadn't been there to encourage him. My advice is to have a look at the five mentors that you need in your life and keep them close.

Serina: Here are the 5 mentors Kath was talking about, which can be found on ideas.ted.com,"The five types of mentors you need in your life":

- *The master of craft*
- *The champion of your cause*
- *The copilot*
- *The anchor*
- *The reverse mentor*

Jass: Yes, I do. He was a really good relationships person within the company, and knew his stuff technically, two things which go hand in hand. He was very humble about what he knew and willing to learn more, and was constantly doing the stuff that was important. He put in the hours when he needed to and made sure he prioritised professional development. He had a plan on what certifications he needed to be successful, identified people he worked wellwith, and built out his networks.

Is where you are now where you thought you would be when you started out?

Kath: Definitely not. In high school, I planned to be in the UK running my own art gallery. Fast forward some years and I'm a mother of two, married, and working in IT security in Australia. If I had told my 18-year-old self that, I would say I was on drugs. You don't know what the future holds. People are so focused on the destinations, which let's be honest, is death. Enjoy the twists and turns and the other shit that happens. Part of you getting and making a difference is the detours, the windy parts that got you there. It's what shapes you as a person and it's those barnacles that you picked up. Why would you fast-track the opportunity to pick up some of that moss?

Jass: Definitely not. I started in assurance and didn't envisage I would end up in a sales role. I enjoyed sales the most out of all the areas I rotated into. If I hadn't had the opportunity to sample other areas, my current role wouldn't have come to fruition. Initially, I thought I was going to be a project manager, as I had studied it at uni. I'm happy I'm not, because it wouldn't have suited me being in a role like that. I lucked into my current area, which is funny, but you never know where your path will go when you take different options and learning opportunities. I liked the people aspect of sales, developing relationships, and of course the lunches. I also like how you are measured by your number, which brings alot of clarity and certainty to what you will be measured by.

Louisa: Absolutely not. I did a physiotherapy degree and I expected that I would be a physio. Now I am in technology, which is the opposite of where I thought I would be. The only thing that was the same was my goal of moving to Australia from England. I went into the workplace just thinking this is a job for now as I need to pay my student debt and bills. I had no clear path planned out. I just wanted to be the best version of me in the workplace. That is still a work in progress. I was going to be a physio, married with two kids and living in England but dreaming of living in Australia. Don't be afraid to change plans from a career perspective. If you come out of uni with an "x" degree and you didn't like it or there were no jobs, get into something that you can use some of the skills you've learnt and see how you go. Don't feel like the world has ended because you didn't become what you thought you would, because you could become something better than you ever imagined.

How do you network?

Kath: I just go up and talk to people. I mean, you and I met in the nail salon when I commented on your nails and look at where we are now. Make sure you pay attention and be present. There's nothing worse than someone remembers you and you don't remember them. I talk about life. Work is work. But I love to know what people do for fun. My job requires me to talk to people all day and do my emailing at night, so there's not a lot of time for hobbies. I have to prioritise what's important to me. I like to know what other people do when they're not at work. You learn a lot by asking that. People love to speak about what they love to do and very quickly we can find common ground, and that's how you build a connection. Also know when to get out. Don't book an hour with people who are super busy when you have nothing to say. If you do run out of time, it's okay to ask for another time to continue on. I've had so many days eaten by awkward grads who don't seem to know what they want from me. Or some even ask me to come up with a list of things that they need to do to be me in the quickest time possible! It's like they are writing a thesis and they are so time poor that they have to find the shortest way there. You have to earn the shit. Understand that. There are certain problems I can help fast-track as a mentor, but learning through the macro twists and turns will be what makes you a better leader.

Jass: I listen first to the person. You need to understand their career path and role. You have to do some background work about why you are actually meeting. The "grad card" is good to meet people, but it's not effective for the long game. Make sure you have a business reason for the catch up, even if it's made up. People struggle with it because it doesn't come naturally. Basically, it's just you getting to know a person, understanding where they're at in their career and how their experiences relate back to yours. It needs to be fruitful for both parties. That's where the best relationships come from. Most of the time, it's actually like the fly on the elephant, where the fly gets all the benefits. Now that I'm more on the other side and mentoring, I'm upskilling myself as I get to see how different people approach things. If you can help or understand both types, you can do a lot. When I mentor people, what I get out of it is I get to expand my knowledge database of what works for different sets of people. Helpsto interact with more people.

Louisa: Personally, I attend events. Since I'm more introverted, they are not comfortable for me, as I much prefer one-on-ones. Developing relationships can take me longer, but it's a quality one because I have gotten to know that person one on one. Do what you're comfortable with when you are at events. You don't have to meet 10 people. Follow up the relationship with a LinkedIn request with a personal message. Over time, it just grows organically. But, of course, remember that someone who is a colleague today can be a customer or a manager tomorrow. Be very consistent with your relationships with people in your network. Don't judge people on what their job is because they're not useful to you today. Everyone can teach you something. Go into it with that open mindedness; I may not know this person, but what can I learn from them?

Chris: As a grad, you have to practise networking, and yes, it is something you can practise. Sometimes at the start, it might not be apparent to you why networking is important, but over time you will see the value. The better you are at your soft skills at networking, the more it will serve you later on when you need to rely on those networks. It can feel like a waste of time when you are talking to people at an event and nothing happens, but it really does add up over time. You never truly know when a conversation will be valuable. It can randomly hit later on, when you are at an event and an opportunity pops up in the least expected way and you can go and pursue that. Conferences are great because you are all there for the same reasons, which is to learn and meet people. The two things I do is try to learn four random things that are relevant to that event or conference. Those four things could resonate with four people at that conference. When you are in a conversation with someone, you slip in one of those things and see what you get back. That is how I get comfortable with random people. You may find a like-minded person through your mutual interest.

What is something you do in every interview you've had?

Kath: I have a list of things I need to know before going in and I'll have those questions ready. I usually ask about the culture, what a typical day looks like, what the travel is like, how flexible are they, and what the vision for my role is. I also ask them to tell me where they see me in five years and ask myself if this aligns to what I want. Ultimately, listen to your gut. If you get answers that make you uneasy or unsure, be cautious. There has never been a time that I had a gut feel that this was wrong, and it wasn't. You earnt a seat in that interview, don't waste it.

Don't be entitled or an asshole, but you do have the opportunity to interview the interviewer. Also, don't forget that sometimes for you to get the ideal role, you have to get some lesser roles to round out your skills before you are ready to take it on.

Jass: At the end of the day, it's a conversation. That may be common advice, but it's amazing how many people have behavioural answers prepared and are very pragmatic about things but forget to have a conversation and let it flow. Create rapport between you and your interviewer, because when you run into trouble, they may help you out with more time to answer or provide some hints. Don't forget that when you are being interviewed at 1pm or 2pm, the person could be starving, they might be cranky because they haven't eaten. If 9am, they may not have had their coffee nor had time to sort out their day. By late afternoon, they may just want to go home. What I'm trying to say is, you need to understand their state of mind when you go in, and work with that.

Louisa: Always treat it as a two-way thing. That is not being arrogant but ask questions back about what you want to know about the team or organisation. Not getting over-excited and then wishing you had asked a question that could have made or broken your decision is important. Using sales techniques, which are asking questions that make you uncomfortable. Do you have any reservations about me? Is there anything in my experience that concerns you—this has been gold when I've gone through it. You can acknowledge that, but then say where your experience can be applicable or parallel to that and tell them what you would do.

"You don't have experience with selling to the bank." "Yes, I agree with that. How I would go about it is x y z." They open up, then you have an opportunity to reassure them about those gaps they have. You should walk out knowing why you haven't gotten the job. If you get it, you know they are comfortable you can overcome the issues—you don't need feedback, as you heard it first. It's hard because you are highlighting your flaws, but facing them on the day is the only chance you can deal with it with them. After the fact, it's too late.

Chris: Get your confidence up. There is nothing worse where you feel like you're on the back foot just before walking into an interview. I have anxiety; everyone does when they walk into an interview. I love ones that are personal, coffee-based, and in a less intimidating and more natural setting. However, whether it's on a couch or in a conference room, I treat them all the same. Be confident that you have the knowledge and the skills for the job, understand who your audience is, and understand the company that you're applying for. I stuffed up so much by not getting these things down. What can I offer a role is a massive one, and I don't hear it enough. "What can you offer us" is a great chance to show them your mindset. If possible, try to develop a relationship with the team or manager so the interview is more organic, and also, you want to know who you are working for. But as a grad, I blindly applied for jobs without asking myself who works there, and what feedback have I had heard on that team? What are other people's experiences on working there? The answer to these questions could save you so much frustration when it's too late and you're in the role. Do the leg work before you apply.

Closing thoughts

So, there you have it guys. I hope these chapters will help you navigate your graduate journey and your career beyond. Serving people underpins everything, and that is why I chose the cover of this book to reflect the canvas strategy, in the hope that you will be reminded every time you look at it.

In an age where everyone is becoming accustomed to a digital world, where most of our communication is online, it is more important than ever to learn how to create real and authentic relationships with people. I believe these skills are in short supply and so if you get the basics right and work on building a personal brand where people trust you with their time and resources, you will have no shortage of opportunities in both your career and personal life.

If you would like further information, questions or advice around anything you have read in this book, please feel free to reach out to me via my website; **www.thegraduatemanifesto.com**

Serina's Book List

Tim Ferriss: Tools of the Titans

Ryan Holiday: The 48 Laws of Power

Tony Robbins: Money: Master the Game

Dr John Demartini: The Gratitude Effect

George Samuel Clason: The Richest Man in Babylon

Napoleon Hill: Think & Grow Rich

Jocko Willink, Leif Babin: Extreme Ownership: How U.S. Navy SEALs Lead and Win

T. Colin Campbell: The China Study

Benjamin Graham: The Intelligent Investor

www.ingramcontent.com/pod-product-compliance
Lightning Source LLC
Chambersburg PA
CBHW051326220526
45468CB00004B/1519